1%

Chance
to Live

How I found the faith
to survive

by Sally-Anne Waudby

with Caroline Brannigan

This book was written, designed
and published in 2012 by

Caroline Brannigan
Richmond, North Yorkshire

By carrying out extensive interviews,
Caroline helps clients to tell the story
they have always meant to write.

www.carolinebrannigan.com
01748 821041

ISBN: 978-0-9568700-9-4

Printed in the UK by the MPG Books Group
Bodmin and King's Lynn

Aly.

This book is dedicated to Simon, Charles and Lucy
and is also a great big thank you to everybody

All The very best

Sally Gunnell x.

Prologue

I was lying very still and felt so tired that I couldn't move. I wanted to open my eyes but it was hard. Muffled sounds seemed far away. When I did manage to lift my heavy eyelids, I saw a maze of wires and tubes. I knew that I was in hospital and that I was ill but not how ill.

My eyes focused on my husband Simon. He was sitting beside my bed with his head in his hands. He had been told that I had suffered a bleed in the brain and there was less than a one per cent chance that I would live. Despite his distress, he had decided that this was a chance, however small, and that his wife would take it.

And I did. It was a long journey back to good health and months before I could go home again but we both had faith. Simon and I have different views on where that faith came from but we both had it.

This is the story of what happened to us and how we travelled the hard and rocky road that followed. It is also the story of my early life, so you can get a picture of the person I am, and of my old adversary - my weight - which is finally being beaten into submission.

Chapter One

I took my first breath at the Duchy House Nursing Home in Harrogate in 1968 where I was delivered by a midwife who turned up in a striped apron and Jesus sandals – there's a sign! My weight was a perfectly respectable 7lb 2oz. I am a born survivor, the downside of which is that my body is always worried there might be a famine round the corner. If it sees food, it wants to eat it just in case no more appears. Unfortunately, it always does appear but these days I try to make it grapes, not gateau.

I grew up on a farm near Wetherby, North Yorkshire with my elder brother. My family kept pigs and sheep and grew potatoes and corn. As a small child I often followed my father as he moved the irrigation pipes among the burgeoning green rows of thirsty potatoes, a seemingly never ending task.

Some of my cousins rode ponies and I wanted to do the same but secretly I always felt a bit scared and suspected that I wasn't a natural, despite good training. Jimbo, a bad tempered Shetland, was my first pony followed by a rather moody grey called Misty. They were stabled in the village because my mother was afraid they might escape on to the A1 which ran by our farm and cause a pile-up.

Pony Club was sheer heaven but I never felt I was as good as my cousins who all seemed to be fantastic riders. At my first Pony Club Camp when I was about 10 my mother was worried and asked my grandmother to check up on me. On arrival she couldn't see me anywhere but found a pile of apple cores under my camp bed, so supposed I was alright.

My weight and I are old enemies. I've always liked my groceries and have been on a diet for 34 years. At my heaviest I tipped the scales at 19 stone 10lb. My brother was pin thin and could eat whatever he wanted with no effect but for me it was different and my mother began to worry about my size early on. I can remember her saying, "We don't do any fizzy drinks, only fruit juice, because Sally-Anne can't drink a lot of those." She would buy boxes of Mars Bars for my father and brother and hide them but I'd sniff them out. My father would say, "We've got a big mouse that lives here."

One day the sleek lines of a Ford Capri came along our drive and in the back was a little golden bundle of fluff. This was my new Corgi puppy who I called Honey and fell in love with. She was a big part of my life. In the corner of the house yard was my den, a hideaway in a garage where I could curl up on an old armchair. Honey and I would go in there and eat whatever I could get my hands on.

My parents worked very, very hard. My mother did all the office side. It used to puzzle her that as a teenager I wasn't very good with my finances because she found figures interesting and I didn't. I'm very proud of my mother, who is a lady who does things with conviction. She brought me up to believe that you have to do things a certain way because it's right and that we all have to take responsibility for our own actions. She doesn't like a hullabaloo like I do.

As I got older I earned a bit of money working on the farm. Potato harvest was great fun as a whole gang of us

3

would follow the old Fergusson potato lifter, singing. For as long as I can remember, I've loved singing and after a while discovered I had a good singing voice. It's not as strong now. To keep me alive after I suffered a bleed in the brain, doctors had to perform a tracheotomy, fitting an oxygen tube through my neck to aid breathing. That's not a great thing for your voice but at least I still have one and anyone hearing me belt out my favourite anthem, "I Will Survive" maybe wouldn't notice any problem.

For me singing was fun and when people tried to drum all the boring theory into me later I couldn't be doing with it and so am not very good technically, though I've sung at the odd wedding. As a child, singing was the only thing I could do easily without any effort. Academia was another matter. The hardest thing I ever did was to learn to read. The only thing I passed with flying colours was my dyslexia test in 1979 at the age of 11. Now I can read, write and spell quite well but as a child it was very tough.

School started for me at the pre-prep at Grosvenor House in Duchy Road, Harrogate to which my brother and I were driven each day by our mother and collected again. I had a ball there, the teachers were great and there were beautiful gardens to play in. Then I moved to Tockwith Primary, two villages away from our home, where I made friends with a girl called Caroline whose mother was a lovely character and rode about in a horse and trap. She'd take us to a little riverside beach to fry sausages and that was wonderful.

Later I headed off to a girls' school, Belmont Birklands in Harrogate, being driven by my mother to Spofforth each morning, then taking the bus under the wing of some older girls my mother had found to keep an eye on me. She was quite concerned about me and got sick of me missing the bus home, wondering when I'd turn up. Even if I was on time she'd have to fish me out of the sweet shop. "Sally-Anne! What are you doing buying sweets!" she'd say.

It was quite a complicated journey, first on a 78b to Harrogate then a connection to Kent Road which we'd often miss, going instead to the sweet booth and walking the rest of the way, munching.

Once the serious learning kicked in, school wasn't quite so much fun. My dyslexia hadn't been identified at that point. My father would sit me down with a book and get frustrated, not understanding why I couldn't do it. At the age of eight I astonished myself by finally managing to write my own name. Lying on my mum and dad's bed, I wrote down the letters and shouted out in delight, "Mummy, I've written my name!" I knew, however, that my brother had been able to do that for years. He was a good boy and I was a pain in the backside, he conformed and I didn't. I know my mother found me difficult. We loved each other to bits but I was a monkey and just wanted life to be fun.

Being asked to read aloud at school was my worst fear but after my dyslexia was recognized I had extra lessons. When I got to grips with the written word I rather enjoyed doing Spoken English and got rather theatrical about reading aloud.

The thing in our family at the age of 11 was to go on to boarding school and I remember my parents being disappointed that they couldn't get me in anywhere because I kept failing the entrance exams. Then my mother heard that Hunmanby Hall near Filey was good at helping children with dyslexia.

By this point I was starting to believe that I was as thick as a brick and part of me still does. I wasn't academic and charmed my way in by arriving at the interview with a basket of beautiful brown eggs. Miss Jefferson, the head, was quite taken with me. I think I amused her. Afterwards came the nerve-wracking wait to hear if I'd been successful. It seemed a last hope.

I'll never forget being picked up from the bus by my mother and sitting in the car when she said, "I've got some good news, Sally-Anne. You've got into Hunmanby." Suddenly I felt normal. I felt like the rest of the family and was ecstatic that I was bright enough to get into a boarding school just like my brother. I wasn't a write-off.

Kitted out in my royal blue check skirt, pale blue or yellow shirt with a peter pan collar, jumper and royal blue blazer, I felt very proud of myself. It appealed to my sense of ostentation. The Sunday suit, which we had to wear to chapel, was also royal blue, a boxy jacket with a skirt on the knee and a camel coat. I don't wear royal blue any more.

New girls were allocated "big sisters" and mine was called Deborah, a fifth former who had written to me all summer before I went so I'd feel I had a friend. The parents went to the hall to hear some kind of speech and Debbie took me off to the gym where all the new girls were playing games.

For all my satisfaction at being accepted at the school, I was starting to feel a bit wobbly. Parents were advised to disappear fairly quickly once we said our goodbyes. I could cry now just thinking about it. For the first time in my life I felt desperate. It was the most heart-wrenching thing I have ever been through. My mother was wearing massive sunglasses which I now realize must have been to disguise the fact that she was crying.

Watching her and my father walking out across the portico, I had to be held back, tears pouring down my face.

Dad wasn't in a very good state either and I heard later that it was a very quiet journey back in the car. On reaching home, my father couldn't eat his tea. But they believed they were doing the right thing.

Later I lay in my cubicle with its little bed, wardrobe and desk and a window looking straight out on to a wall. That first night was terrible as reality struck and it was horrendous. All night I was up and down to the house mistress. She was fairly no-nonsense. It was the stiff upper lip mentality. As the days went on, I was backwards and forwards to my "big sister" Debbie and drove her and all her friends mad. One evening I went to her room and another girl shoved me out again, telling me I had to get on with it.

In my heart I knew I couldn't do anything about the turn my life had taken. Being at boarding school was part of being a success so I just had to get on with it. Slowly I came to terms with my new life at school where I found many other farmers' daughters were among the pupils. A girl in the year above, nick-named Meggie, was the daughter of a friend of my father and I had been told she would be looking out for me but didn't meet her until later.

We were playing British Bulldogs on the South Lawn near the ha-ha. One day, a couple of weeks after I arrived, I heard someone shout, "Meggie!" and realized this must be her. Despite the fact that I towered over her at that stage, I went up to her and said, "Your daddy says you've got to look after me". She did and has done so ever since, spanning 30 years.

My mother wrote often, telling me news from the farm like how many eggs the hens had laid. Two pay phones, one in the dining room and one in Blakeston Wing, had been installed for pupils' use and I was never off them. I'd dial my home number, shout either "Dining room!" or "Blakeston!" before the pips went and my parents would ring me back. I never bothered asking them to come and get me because I knew they never would.

I didn't see my parents again for about a month until exeat when I could go home for the weekend. Returning to school that first Sunday night was very difficult but I got used to it all. It became bearable.

A strict routine of meals, lessons, prep and sports took over and stopped me from thinking too much. We had to hand-wash our own knickers and socks and that was pretty grim. Everything else went to the laundry.

Food was served on a cafeteria system so you could have salad or chips and of course I chose chips. A big island was piled with bread and raspberry jam and you could take what you liked and I did. I think I ate my way through my childhood and, as I got older, my increasing weight was a constant worry for my mother. I didn't like being fat but it was comfort food all the time. Whenever I felt sad, I ate. Because I knew what it was like to be unhappy, I was always the one to put my arm round the person who was being bullied and comfort them.

The home of one of my friends was close by, whereas mine was quite a long drive away, and her mother would take us out sometimes at the weekend. It was a relief to get out, despite the grounds being beautiful.

Perhaps I was the despair of the teachers who had to write my reports for I had very little self discipline but I got on alright with most of the other girls because I think they thought I was noisy and fun. I couldn't wait for the beginning of the holidays when my father's car would draw up outside and whisk me away. Holidays were spent helping on the farm, riding and playing with my good friends the Listers across the road. Every day I'd bike down to the village to where my pony was stabled. By now this was a Connemara called Gorse, a 14h 2 dun mountain and moorland mare sturdy enough to carry a big child. She was beautiful, well bred and at last I started to achieve the kind of success at shows I'd longed for, pushing to the back of my mind the nagging belief that some other kid could have done really well on her. I always felt that I didn't quite make the grade.

I spent five years at Hunmanby Hall and in the end quite enjoyed it, especially when I got a boyfriend, a friend of my brother's who was a bit older and would take me out from school now and again. But by the age of 15 I was desperate to leave. I'd got friendly with a lot of girls in the year above and when they left before me I was deeply unhappy and wanted out as soon as possible.

You don't like doing things you find difficult and I found academic subjects difficult. I came out with a handful of O-levels and CSEs and now wish I'd worked harder at school but at the time I just didn't get it.

Finally, when I was 16, my last day arrived. My boyfriend rolled up the school driveway in a Range Rover and pulled up in front of the portico where all the girls were waiting to leave. I liked him very much but Range Rovers were the real love of my life. I'd driven cars round the farm a bit and knew how to make them go, so I begged him to let me take the wheel as far as the end of the drive.

We loaded all my belongings into the back and it was a great moment to be driving myself away from school with all the girls running beside us. Down the drive we went, out of the gates and I drove all the way home. I went down the

Malton by-pass, where I tried a bit of overtaking, and then through York. I think my boyfriend fell asleep. Everything was fine until we were almost back when I passed a friend of my parents. By the time I got home he was on the phone to my mother, who was remarkably sanguine about it.

A-levels were clearly not for me and my parents had to puzzle out what best to do with me next, finally settling on Eggleston Hall. Eggleston is a rather romantic-looking Georgian mansion surrounded by large and beautiful gardens up in the peace of Teesdale, not far from Barnard Castle. Today it's a private home, though the public can visit the grounds, but used to be what was quaintly known as a finishing school where girls could be polished up into good wife material. It was either that or be a Norland Nanny, for I loved children, and since Meggie was going to Eggleston, I voted for that.

Chapter Two

When I arrived at Eggleston Hall in 1984 it was the end of an era. Few young women today think that fancy French cooking and flower arranging are essential qualifications in life and I must have been one of the last to be preened in this way. Later the house was used in the reality TV show Ladette to Lady which tried to turn rough diamonds into sparkling gems. I think I was one of the very first ladettes because I was pretty noisy and liked to have a laugh.

No terrifying entrance exams or interviews this time and I liked cooking so I thought I'd be fine. Most of the other girls came from the Home Counties. Meggie and I sat in our pleasant surroundings sipping tea with our parents that first day, surrounded by all these smart Southerners, and wondered what we'd let ourselves in for. There were quite a few Cordelias.

Despite the other girls being so far from home, they had society connections all over the place and before long were swanning off to shooting parties and country house weekends. It was amazing how swiftly they got themselves settled into the North Yorkshire/County Durham sets. Meggie and I thought we knew a lot of people but these were another type completely. They came to call us "Miss Yorkshire" in their plummy accents. Every weekend we

11

could go home and on Fridays my father would drive on rather tortuous roads to collect me. By the end of the first week I'd started to drop my Yorkshire accent and was working on a rather cut glass variety. My father picked me up on it straightaway. "I'm not sending you there to learn to speak differently!" So I gave up on that. It's always better to be yourself.

The first day we were there we had to pluck and dress a grouse shot the day before on the moor and that put off a lot of the Southerners whereas Meggie and I were fine. We ate everything we cooked. Lamb Breton, meringues, vacherins, crème a la vanille, which is French custard, pastries and all kinds of sauces - I can still make a good sauce. Everything was Cordon Bleu with a lot of cream and butter and I loved it.

We'd trot round the garden to cut foliage for our flower arranging in elaborate L-shaped and triangular patterns, listen to experts telling us how to choose wines and, in a cursory nod to the times, were offered some secretarial skills. Needlework was another of the Jane Austen style accomplishments we were required to learn and by the end of the course had to have produced a ball gown.

It was all fairly sedate and nothing like the TV series. The only really ladette-style thing I ever did was a bit of joyriding. On my 17th birthday I'd got a provisional licence and was desperate to be on my own wheels, especially being stuck out in the wilds of Teesdale. Meggie had already passed and I was madly jealous of her green Polo. One morning when she was still in bed I pestered her to take me out but instead she just handed me the keys and told me to go on my own.

I'd driven cars around the farm so knew how to make

them go and set off through the gates of Eggleston Hall feeling wildly free and scared stiff. As I pulled out, a wagon came thundering down the hill towards me and I had to put my foot down to avoid being flattened. My heart was still thumping as I took a little run around the lanes, then headed back thinking, "Quit while you're ahead."

Although I was happy, for I managed to have a lot of fun, all Eggleston did was turn you into a glorified housewife and that's not the kind of person I am. After my year there was up, I came away with my Eggleston Hall certificate but not the coveted Cordon Bleu diploma which some girls achieved.

I came home at the age of 17 with no clear idea of what I wanted to do and gladly took up the job my father had secured for me nearby with Wright Rain, an irrigation company, to work in the office, though I don't think I was particularly good at it.

I was never without a job but had lots of them and soon was off to Wetherby to work as nanny to a gorgeous little boy, driving there legally having passed my driving test. My first car was a lovely Mini Metro called the Yellow Peril. The day after I passed my test I crashed it taking a flask to my father who was working at another farm. Bare-footed on a blazing hot day and going much too fast, I hit a white fiesta van belonging to contractors working for my father. Unhurt but absolutely devastated, I stepped out guiltily to hear his words, "I knew this was going to happen. At least you're alright. We can fix the car but we can't fix you." Despite this baptism of fire, the Yellow Peril became notorious on the roads around North Yorkshire.

When I was 21 I decided to become a hairdresser but couldn't face all that hair washing that apprentices have to do so went to a six-month hair academy course in Leeds but life in a real salon wasn't the glamour I'd hoped for. I was earning a pittance and decided it wasn't for me.

Flicking through The Lady magazine, I was tempted by a job in London which sounded too good to be true, I handed in my notice and headed South, probably because of the white Golf convertible offered. It was a palatial, smart house in Hampstead with top-notch accommodation for me. They were very keen to have me to save on using Prue Leith to do their dinner parties. With 10 or 12 guests expected, I'd meet my employer at Harrods food hall, having been driven there by the chauffeur in a Rolls-Royce. No expense was spared. Through my contacts I gathered young men and women to wait at table. My employers also loved my Eggleston flower arrangements around the house and even asked me to do them in the husband's head office.

August was St. Tropez, winter was skiing from their Swiss mountain chalet. A Range Rover and a Golf were kept in Geneva permanently for the hour drive to the chalet. On my first visit, their 10-year-old son attached the skis to the car roof. I assumed he had done it dozens of times before. Driving down the motorway in heavy snow, people kept flashing their lights at us until we heard one shout, "Your skis have come off the roof!"

My boss had me running down the motorway looking for skis and was uncomplimentary about me, to say the least. "I'm really sorry but I've never done this before," I said. We never saw the skis again. The road down to the chalet was very steep and I was a nervous wreck every time I did that journey. But I was well paid, had a swish car, saw some exciting places and didn't feel in any way exploited. Apart from our spat over the skis, they were both very nice to me. We went to the opening night of Disneyland in Paris which was fabulous. We'd also go to Cape Town because some of the production for her husband's company was carried out there.

Every weekend saw me speeding up the M1 back to Yorkshire, my friend Rachel sitting white-faced beside me. She worked as a nanny a couple of streets away. I don't drive like that now! The bright lights of London held no fascination for me. I couldn't see me walking into any of the famous nightclubs. Why? Because I was fat. I thought I'd have got laughed at. I felt very comfortable in Yorkshire where everyone knew and accepted me. It's one thing being a party girl in Yorkshire, another being a party girl in London where you had to be stick thin. I wasn't. I was a good size 16 to 18.

The only clubs I went to were gay clubs with my friend Robert, who was gay, and Lucy, a Yorkshire friend who, like me, wasn't. Madame JoJo's was a favourite and we got the giggles until we cried, thinking what our fathers would say if they could see us. The men looked like goddesses – not gods! – in women's clothes and even swimsuits. It was an unthreatening environment where we weren't being judged.

Lucy and I have both battled our weight. Sometimes we try to tot up how many stones we've put on, lost and put on again over the years. Today I'm well on the way to getting to my target at last because I feel I've been given a second chance to live and want to make the most of it. But it hasn't been easy.

After two or three years in London I wanted a change. It all sounds very glamorous but was in fact hard work. I used to write my resignation letter then leave it in a drawer for lack of anything to go to but eventually left for another family in Yorkshire where I stayed for a couple of years. I reached the age of 24 still asking myself, what more is there to life? Fortunately for me, I was just about to meet the man I was to marry. Simon Waudby was an uncut diamond who turned into a 24 carat. We have been to hell and back together – and to Hull Hospital and back! We've survived.

The Bachelors and Spinsters Ball was an important event on the society calendar and I found myself on the organizing committee. That year it was held in a marquee on a farm near Escrick, York.

My job on the night was to check tickets at the door but because of my dyslexia we got in a terrible muddle. Simon's brother Angus arrived (I didn't know who he was then) and he and I had words on the door because I queried his ticket.

It was a cracking night. At about 1am we served a huge breakfast – sausage, egg, bacon, beans, mushrooms, cheese – and I was spooning cheese on to plates. Up came a man I'd never met before with lovely blue, twinkly eyes. Simon, being the cheeky chappie he is, said, "Give me another spoonful of that and I'll take you for a dance." And so I did.

Unbeknown to me, he'd seen me earlier surrounded by a crowd of men, not because I was everyone's idea of the perfect woman but because they thought I was a laugh. I always had plenty of men who were friends. Simon had told his brother, "I think I'm going to ask her for a dance." And Angus replied, "You don't want to ask her, she's a stuck up cow. I had a right do with her on the door." Luckily for us, he wasn't put off.

Simon is a lovely chap and was very attentive so I was interested in getting to know him better but decided he'd have to get rid of the gold necklace he was wearing. He asked me to a 21st birthday party the following night but

I had been brought up not to attend an event to which I hadn't been invited directly so declined but we met on the Sunday and went to the cinema. He held my hand all night, which I thought was very gentlemanly. The fact that I have a lazy eye didn't stop him thinking I was lovely.

After meeting me, Simon's father told him, apparently, "You want to crack on with her, she's a nice girl." Simon was an agricultural contractor and, despite being a very hard worker, wasn't the kind of chap that perhaps my parents would have preferred. It didn't matter a hoot to me. He'd grown up on a farm but it had been sold and he was adamant that one day he would have somewhere of his own. He's never had anything handed to him on a plate but I've never had to want for anything since I married him.

I'd once said to him that if anyone ever proposed to me, I'd like it to be at Runswick Bay where my grandmother had a house and I had spent many happy holidays. One weekend we were there on the beach and I thought Simon had fallen because suddenly he was on his knees. He looked up and asked me to do him the greatest honour of becoming his wife. I knew he loved me absolutely unconditionally and said yes straightaway. He said, "Tomorrow we'll go and get a ring and you can have anything you like." And I did, a beautiful ruby.

My parents already knew of our engagement because Simon had been to see my father to ask for my hand in marriage. Apparently my father said, "Of course you can but you know what she is – a handful!" Obviously it didn't put him off.

I was a bit wild and sometimes drank too much. For the last five years I haven't drunk at all, partly to try to lose weight, but back then I was having a great time knocking back vodka. I went to the Wetherby Show Ball with my parents. There was a grand piano and I said to my cousin, who is a good pianist, "You play and I'll sing." We jumped up and did the Elaine Paige number "Midnight". I was absolutely blathered, sang very badly and my mother went home in disgust. The president intervened and took the microphone off me with the words, "Young lady, you have not been invited to sing." That put me in my place, though I got a round of applause.

At the show lunch the following day, my godmother came up to me and said, "As your godmother I have to ask you not to drink as much as you have been doing." My friends used to say they had some of the best times of their lives with me – and some of the worst. Both my dad and Simon's were happy about the engagement but our mothers less so. Despite this, my mother put an awful lot of effort into our wedding and I had a lovely, lovely day.

I ignored vaguely guilty feelings in my subconscious that in some way I was letting my parents down. I loved Simon and knew he was as sound as a pound. If he was a dog, he'd be a Labrador. Whenever we visited anyone, within a few minutes it would be either their child or their dog on his knee. My children have a wonderful father. If I hadn't married him and had his support, I wouldn't be here today.

By this time I'd set up my own cleaning business, Done and Dusted, put out flyers and had T-shirts made for the four or five people I employed. Believe it or not, I was a very good cleaner and even my mother approved because I was earning a living. That business evolved into Clean-A-Matic for carpet and upholstery cleaning.

For some time I'd had my own home and when Simon and I decided to marry I sold it. Simon sold some land he owned and we bought a house together. The night before the wedding I celebrated with my bridesmaids, then back at home my father opened some champagne.

We kept going down to the cellar to get more. Unfortunately my mother found the empties in a bin liner under the kitchen table the next morning. "You are a silly, silly girl," she told me as I nursed my hangover. Happily, by three o' clock when I had to be at the church I was feeling better.

We were married at Hunsingore Church in June 1997 and the reception was held in a marquee at home. Instead of wedding cars we had a fleet of my favourite Range Rovers. It was a fabulous day, despite the fact that when I said "I do" there was a crack of thunder.

Before this, Yorkshire Life had been looking for someone to write a society diary and for a while my friend Wendy and I had been compiling Sally-Anne's Diary about all the important functions that went on, including weddings, but my mother wouldn't allow a magazine photographer at mine. I think I was always a bit of an embarrassment to her. "It's not going to be turned into a circus," she told me. There was always chaos and confusion when I was around.

At the end of the day I went upstairs to change, then looked out of the window at a sea of happy faces and threw out my bouquet. It was a wonderful moment.

And so Simon and I set off on married life together. He has been a far better husband than I have been a wife to him. I've said some terrible things to him. I hardly ever had a meal ready on time and was disorganized in the house, it was shambolic really, but he never moaned. I'm no Annie Sugden and haven't turned out to be the farmer's wife perhaps he hoped for.

Chapter Three

Driving through the village of Tholthorpe one day, I spotted a for sale sign being hammered in outside a gorgeous cottage called The Laurels. I drove straight to the agent's, we viewed it that evening and soon it was ours. For some reason, Simon said, "We'll only be here a year" and we were, to the week.

Our next home was Ivy House Farm. It came up for sale in the village of Flawith and tempted us because it had a smallholding with some outbuildings. It was like The Darling Buds of May. Simon's business was growing and it was awkward where we were having a tractor and machinery parked outside the house. Ivy House Farm had a lovely farmhouse, even my mother was impressed, and it was our home for 15 years. We had some very happy times there and some very sad ones.

Throughout my life I always knew something was going to happen to me. I had a privileged childhood and had led a charmed life to some degree but at the back of my mind was this deep-seated feeling that something nasty was waiting.

I had no idea what that would be. When I had my son Charles in2001, I thought I was too big and unfit and was terrified that my fate would be to die in childbirth. But I didn't. People have popped up at various times of my life when I've needed them and I like to call them my angels.

Just before my baby was due, the wife of our vicar called round. I confided my fears to her and we prayed together that I would be looked after. That gave me strength to survive 55 hours of labour ending in an emergency caesarean. You wouldn't put a dog through it. Simon was there holding my hand all through. But at the end I held my son in my arms, his head a mass of dark hair, and how wonderful was that!

Up until this point I'd been a typical English Christian, getting married in church but usually thinking of God only when I needed help. Now I began to feel a need to get to know Him better.

However, my new baby and our busy working lives took up most of my thoughts. Our daughter Lucy arrived in 2004 and this time it was a planned caesarean. I felt completely safe with no sense of foreboding and everything went well, apart from hearing the surgeon say, "I hope I don't have another one of those today!" I have always thought she meant it was hard to get my baby out of my fat tummy. But maybe it wasn't that at all.

Back home and now with two children, it was a very hectic time, though I had au pairs to help. Our farm was busy as we'd started rearing geese and getting hundreds of them ready for that first Christmas was a task. For years since then I've spent every Christmas up to my nose in feathers and insides. At Eggleston I'd learned how to dress a grouse and these were just bigger. A lot of my friends are surprised I do it but why wouldn't I?

I was still running my carpet and upholstery cleaning business, which was jolly hard work, and was looking for something different. Suddenly something came up out of the blue. As a child I would go to watch my cousins at sports day at Cundall Manor School not far from where we now live and hoped that I'd be able to send my children there. When Charles was old enough he joined the nursery. I met some very nice people there including the then head teacher Peter Phillips and his lovely wife Sarah.

In 2005 one of the other parents was holding a girlie evening at her home where someone was coming in to sell things and I went but really so I could have a nosy at the house. I'd heard it was new but built in a traditional manner. To my surprise I found myself interested in the talk about the lotions and potions on display, called Forever Living Products. By the time it was over, I'd bought a business in a box – a box of products to sell myself - and I thought, what have I done?

They're all based on aloe vera and boost your immune system, help your joints and skin, are anti-oxidant and are your internal doctor. As well as a drinking gel, there is toothpaste, soap, shower gel, shampoo, moisturizer, make-up – everything you can think of. I use loads of it and people say how well I look. I feel it has helped me to recover from the terrible illness I suffered.

I knew I was a born saleswoman as long as I believed in what I was selling. I wanted to do something with people and with Forever Living Products you can build up a team to work with through network marketing, going to people's homes, to fairs and so on. I'll walk up to anyone and tell them about it because I think everyone should have the chance to benefit.

Simon was great about it. I went home that night with my box of tricks for which I'd paid nearly £200 and he just said go for it. Quite quickly I became a manager and then he wasn't so keen because it took me away from home, though he was great at looking after the children and holding the fort. One of the nicest things anyone ever said to me came about because of my work with Forever Living Products which was, "You may not have a degree but you've got something more important – charisma" and that was a great confidence boost. I felt I had to use it.

Forever Living Products were good for my body but I was also looking for something which would be good for my soul. Through Cundall Manor I made friends with a wonderful woman called Ruth. The first time I walked into her house I saw three hearts hanging from the ceiling with a word on each: Jesus Loves You. Beforehand someone else had whispered to me, "They're very religious you know!" People who themselves might tick the "Christian" box on a form can be very hostile towards those who aren't afraid to show their strong Christian beliefs. Instead of being hostile, I was intrigued. I knew there was a gap in my life but didn't know what I was looking for.

Ruth and her husband Dan invited me to go on an Alpha course in Sowerby, an introduction to Christianity with sessions held once a week for 10 weeks. I walked into the village hall with Ruth to find about 25 other people of all ages there and felt a bit nervous. After getting to know each other a bit over a meal cooked by volunteers, there was a talk or video about different aspects of Christianity, then we broke into small groups to talk. When they said, "Let's pray together," I was terrified and felt very self-conscious. There was no kneeling or hands pressed together, just closed eyes, but I found myself cringing. I thought, "I'm not sure about this."

To my surprise, I found myself there again the following week and kept on going. One session was held near Pickering and that was an amazing day with music and singing and I felt the room was full of the Holy Spirit. People gave their testimonials about how Christianity had changed their lives. On leaving, I felt as if I was walking on air. It wasn't wham, bam and flashing lights but I felt as if my cup was overflowing. It was as if I had finally arrived at a place I'd been searching for.

That was the moment when things changed for me. Ever since then I have felt as if I have been carried and that whatever happens I can get through it. People said dismissively, "She's got religion" as if it was a disease, or "This isn't the Sally-Anne I know". I began to feel a bit ashamed. They started to greet me with, "Hello Sally-Anne, how's God?" and I'd say, "Why don't you ask him yourself?" My mother didn't approve. I think she thought, "For goodness sake, why can't she do it quietly?" That's the English way. Christianity is turning up every Sunday in a hat and polishing the pews. Anything more and they think you're a nutter. A few people were pleased for me, even though they knew it wasn't for them. Others just labelled me a God-botherer.

I knew bashing people over the head with The Bible was no solution or they'd just run a mile. You can't start bellowing about Jesus. Simon says, "A leopard doesn't change its spots" and points out that sometimes I don't do very Christian things. I admit I do let myself down occasionally but I've got a really good heart, it's just been bashed a bit.

I enjoy a traditional service but also like a bit of variation so I go to two churches, one of which is what detractors call "happy clappy" which just means we sing moderns hymns and it's less formal. I don't understand why these derogatory terms are used when no-one is forced to go. Some older people find it difficult to accept any changes, like swapping the organ for a guitar or swaying along to the music in the pews. I was next to one elderly lady who confided, "I can't get used to this swaying!" and I just replied, "Oooh, you get swaying!" and she did.

There is a great fear of happy clappiness. We're buttoned up in this country yet many people who call themselves Christians blaspheme. When that happens I say, "Do you mind? He's a friend of mine!" I picked my mother up on it and she said, "Sally-Anne, I've been saying it for years and I'm not going to stop just because you're running around waving a tambourine!" I just pray for her and hope that one day she'll understand why I have such strong faith. I'm not saying she should be like this.

Chapter Four

Any farmer will tell you that you usually get only one chance in a lifetime to buy the land next-door to you and we'd already passed up twice on that very thing. When the land came on the market for a third time Simon said, "We've got to go for this. We'll never get the opportunity again." It was a beautiful spot with views for miles and I'd often walked our dogs across there and thought how lovely it was and this seemed the right thing to do.

So we bought the land and there followed the protracted and difficult task of getting planning permission to build a farm there. That was a battle but eventually we received outline permission for buildings then a farmhouse, though that was only the first step.

Life was busy with our young family, the farm and now this new project. But then life suddenly reared up and smacked us in the face with something terrible and everything changed. I had always had a mysterious fear that something nasty was in store for me but when I began to feel ill in September 2007, I had no idea how bad things were going to get.

I was getting blinding headaches. My doctors were fantastic but at first sight thought it was a virus. The pain didn't go away and I spent much of the day lying in darkened rooms. Simon didn't know what to do for the best. I remember going to my mother's and collapsing on the floor. They took me to Harrogate Hospital but after more tests I was allowed home. My mother says she will never forgive herself for coming away from the hospital without a proper diagnosis but how was anyone to know how bad things were? Nothing was showing up at that time.

The following day she took me to the optician to get prescription sunglasses so I could stand the light. I have only snippets of memory of the terrible time that followed when my life hung by a thread and so it is now to Simon that I must turn to help me tell my story.

Simon: It all started on September 17th 2007. We'd been out for dinner the night before and in the morning Sally-Anne bent down to the washing machine and, bang! instant pain. I'd gone off to a meeting and got a call from her saying how ill she felt and that she'd taken some painkillers. In the evening I took her to the doctor because she had suffered more severe pain. She was given more painkillers. Then she began hallucinating. I took her to her mother's so she could get some peace and quiet, for our children were only six and three at the time and didn't understand.

Our hostess from the dinner party that previous night heard that the doctor had quizzed us on what Sally-Anne had eaten and exclaimed in horror, "F***! Have I killed her?" This gives us both a good laugh now but everything was far from funny at the time.

Things got no better and on the 19th and Sally-Anne was sent for an MRI scan which showed no abnormalities. On the 20th she had a lumber puncture which was normal. They call these negative results "blind". We would never for one

27

minute blame anyone because nothing was showing up and everything was done that was possible to trace the problem. In 99 per cent of cases, the first test would have shown up the bleed. An earlier diagnosis would have improved her chances but it was just one of those things.

The following words were written by Sally-Anne on September 20th 2007 in York Hospital. She wanted them read out at her funeral if she did not come through surgery.

Yesterday we thought we were home and dry, thinking the MRI scan was clear. Today I still have to have a lumber puncture to see if there are any traces of blood in my spine. If so, there has been bleeding in my brain and I will be transferred to Hull. So yes, I am scared, not so much about the needle but the outcome. My grandfather used to say, "Hull, hell and Halifax". Knowing my luck, I will die having surgery in Hull. Not ideal. Hopefully you won't get to hear my words but me being me, I wanted to be prepared while I am fairly calm and positive.

Today, my greatest achievements have been my children. How lucky have I been to produce two fabulous little people, Charles and Lucy! They are our life and the thought of not being around to watch them grow up into adults makes me feel distraught. If that happens, I will regret all the time I have spent away from the home trying to carve a career in order to create a nice life for them. Really, I would have been much better being at home. My time should, and if I get the chance, be spent in the home with nothing more to worry about other than us, no work for me other than looking after my family. If you get to hear these words, I want you all to be a part of their lives for ever. Talk about me as though I were still around and answer all their questions. Promise me to love and listen to them, tell them about me and how proud I would have been of them and was of them.

Simon: By now I was getting very worried. Sally-Anne was having violent head pains, hallucinating, being sick and couldn't eat. Our GP came out with all these test results which offered no clues at all to what was happening. A bleed in the brain was an obvious possibility but none of the usual signs were showing. We could see that Sally-Anne was going downhill badly, sleepy all the time and not with it at all. She could still talk to me but found it difficult because of the pain. All the curtains were closed because she couldn't bear the light.

In the end she collapsed at her parents' house and was taken to Harrogate Hospital by ambulance where yet more tests produced yet more puzzles and no answers, so it was home again with all the same symptoms turning her life into a nightmare.

By now word had got round that Sally-Anne wasn't getting better, that this wasn't some bug which would clear up as mysteriously as it had arrived. A friend came round with beef tea which was a traditional cure-all. It was kind but things had progressed much further than that.

As a bleak September turned to October, the doctor tried some pick-me-up pills which sent Sally-Anne very high. She rang up her friend Ruth saying she was going to start a band and save the world, talking complete gobbledygook. After finishing the dose, Sally-Anne plunged down once more into a trough but a day or two later seemed a bit better and managed to eat a little. I began to hope that the doctors had been right, that this was a virus and at last Sally-Anne's body had learned how to fight it off. But by the following day she was in severe pain again and had lost interest in everything. The GP came out and sent us again to York Hospital that evening where she was admitted. That was the Friday. The children were taken care of by a friend.

A young doctor there repeated all the tests they could think of, including another lumber puncture, which again came back blind. About one o' clock in the morning he came to see me. "What do you think's the matter?" I asked. He looked at me and said, "I haven't got a bloody clue." I thought that was a good, honest answer for a doctor to make. He didn't try to fluff it over and I didn't want any more bull about thinking it's a virus or this or that.

About two o' clock I went home to try to get some sleep in the hope that there would be better news later. The children were staying with friends and were starting to wonder when life would return to normal. That was to be a very long time in the future, though none of us knew it then. I had to keep telling them that Mummy wasn't well and was in hospital having tests. Throughout all our traumas, I don't think they ever realized how near the edge she was. They were too young to handle that kind of information.

It was just a few hours later that we at last reached the tipping point. That was Saturday October 6th. At six o'clock in the morning the phone rang and I heard the doctor say, "We've done some tests, Mr Waudby, can you come into the hospital?" That was the worst moment of all for me. They don't ring you up at that time and ask you to come in straightaway if it isn't serious. They weren't going to say she had an in-growing toenail and would be out by lunchtime.

Bleary-eyed and fearful, I drove through the early morning light of Saturday into York. I was met by the consultant who told me, "Your wife is extremely ill. She's had a bleed on the brain." A short time later I was in my car again, following in the wake of an ambulance which had sped off, blue lights flashing, taking Sally-Anne to Hull where they could offer more specialized care.

There was no point asking why they hadn't found out sooner. Even the CT scan and the MRI scan had shown nothing. It was a very small but potentially lethal bleed which had hidden away very cleverly while doing its damage. Eventually things had deteriorated enough for the tests to pick it up. From being clear before, there was a definite blackness showing.

Sally-Anne, lying in a high dependency room, had little idea of what was going on. She was full of different drugs and was hallucinating. She had endured so much pain and had slept so little in the weeks leading up to this.

At Hull they told me that a third of people suffering a bleed in the brain survive and recover, a third don't come out alive from the operating theatre and a third are badly affected afterwards. With all their experience, my opinion is that they didn't think she'd see the weekend out.

I rang Sally-Anne's brother Simon who was our point of contact with her side of the family to tell him the grim and shocking news that his sister had suffered an aneurism. An aneurism occurs when a vein begins to leak. The best way to describe it is like an inner tube. If you blow it up too tight it can develop a blister on the side which becomes a weak point. Anyone can have them, never knowing, and have no problems at all. But for the unluckiest ones, these weak points can suddenly go and take you out completely - lights out, that's it.

They could not operate until the Monday morning. The

first operation they carried out was to put a coil into the brain to plug the hole and stop the bleed. I sat in the waiting room. Eventually the doctor arrived and said, "It's been a big success" and showed me on a diagram what they'd done.

Despite the seriousness of Sally-Anne's illness, I began to feel more positive. For me, the two worst moments were the telephone call from York Hospital and the news on arrival that they had found out what was wrong. After that, as my wife lay in intensive care, I thought, "She's a young person with two children and if she was going to die she would have done so by now." Even when things got so much worse after that, I never gave up hope.

At that stage I was going backwards and forwards between hospital and home where friends and family were helping to keep things together. Our friend Wendy was one of many stars. Having left Sally-Anne in a fairly reasonable condition on the Tuesday evening, I rang the hospital at ten o'clock before going to bed to see how she was and was told she had gone downhill very badly. "Mr Waudby," said the doctor, "things are not going very well and we have taken her down to theatre. There's no point in rushing over because she'll be in there for five or six hours."

Remembering all this still brings a lump to my throat. I'd run a bath and that had gone cold but I dipped in anyway and, after calling relatives, headed off with my two brothers who were with me that night. Hull seemed eerie as we sped through the deserted streets.

In the early hours of Wednesday morning October 10th 2007, our families began gathering at the hospital. I called it Black Wednesday. There was nothing we could do but wait in the room set aside for relatives of patients who are very seriously ill. In the operating theatre extraordinary things were happening. Fluid had built up in Sally-Anne's brain and the surgeon cut a "bone flap" in her skull about two inches by three to release it. This "door" of bone was then inserted into Sally-Anne's stomach where the body would look after it as live tissue until it was safe to close the door once more.

Despite being the middle of the night, this highly specialized unit was a busy place with trolleys being wheeled in and out. I remember one going past with a fleet of nurses and doctors buzzing round, then one of those jump-starter machines you see on the TV programme Casualty. At first it didn't register with me that this was Sally-Anne.

The surgeon walked in. You can tell by their faces how things are going, how solemn they are. Not in so many words, they basically said that was it. It was the end and just a matter of time.

"What are her chances?" I asked. "Will she die?"

"I can't say."

"Is it 50-50?"

"No."

"Ten, five, two, one per cent?"

The answer eventually came back, "Less than one per cent."

If he'd been honest he'd have said she'd live another hour or two and that they'd put money on it that she'd die. But he would have been wrong because you can never say never. To me, that "less than one per cent" was like winning the lottery. We had a chance, no matter how small, and I knew Sally-Anne would take it.

The rest of the family believed this was the time to make their last goodbyes to Sally-Anne and urged me to do the same. My brother Angus told me, "You have to accept it, she's going to die." Even if she survived, she would be a vegetable. Despite the fact that Sally-Anne was lying there unconscious, wired up, piped up and full of drugs, I said, "No, she isn't."

My other brother Richard felt just the same as me. "She's a fighter. She isn't going to die," he said. The others looked on us with pity. I can't remember what I said to Sally-Anne when I went in but it certainly wasn't goodbye. I kept mentioning Charles and Lucy to her. I phoned our friend Emma for support and over the next three days she, Richard and I made sure that at least one of us was at the hospital, just in case. Things were extremely tense as the situation was very precarious with Sally-Anne fighting for her life. Her life hung by a fine thread and it would not take much to break it.

I knew how important Sally-Anne's religious belief was to her, even though it wasn't for me. I'd been brought up in the traditional CofE, that you go two or three times a year and try to do your bit for the local church. We're all different and I call the more evangelical ones God botherers but Sally-Anne had got a lot out of it.

So I phoned her friends Ruth and Dan who had introduced her to the Alpha Course. I didn't feel it was my choice, it was Sally-Anne's choice. Dan at that time was preparing to be ordained and they came straightaway, despite having a baby of only eight weeks, and prayed over Sally-Anne.

Sally-Anne: When I was on the life support machine and given a less than one per cent chance of survival, Simon didn't quite know what to do but he didn't want the hospital priest to be with me, he wanted someone who knew me. I know my mother found it very difficult to see them praying over my head and I can understand that but it's what I would have wanted, had I been aware of what was going on. Simon got it absolutely spot on.

We don't agree on where faith comes from but we both had it. Mine comes from Jesus and I firmly believe that Jesus saw Simon's faith and acted on it. My husband was like a general. He went into battle for me and won.

Chapter Five

Simon: Back in Flawith, friends and neighbours were gathering around Ivy House Farm, unable to believe the terrible news from Hull. Everyone held their breath, waiting for the devastating blow which they felt was sure to follow. But it didn't. Going from nearly pegging it, Sally-Anne's condition remained static for a couple of days.

There was always someone, a friend or relative, with her. I was nipping backwards and forwards to home, making sure everything was as well as it could be with the children and on the farm. It was a crucial time on the farm, with crops gathered and new ones needing to be sown and animals to be fed. My brothers and other farmers pitched in. Kristian, who works for us, and his wife Carina were a huge support. Kristian kept things going so I didn't have to worry.

His phone never stopped because I'd brief him on how Sally-Anne was so he could be an information hub for the concerned community. He told me there were a lot of teary people about the village, hugging each other. One day he said he never got out of the yard because the phone didn't stop ringing.

Our good friend Emma and her husband Martin moved into our home with their children, who are great friends with our son and daughter, to give Charles and Lucy some stability rather than having different people coming and going. They stayed for about a fortnight. Though we had tried to keep the seriousness of the situation from the children, obviously word had got around and little ears had been wagging.

I never thought Sally-Anne would die. From being next-door to death, she began to pick up a bit. By the end of that week it became apparent to everyone that she wasn't going to leave us but it was to be a very, very long journey back with plenty of ups and downs.

With a sigh of relief, I vacated the little room they'd given me because that was for relatives of patients not expected to make it and I drove to the hospital each day, a three-hour round trip. I wanted to be around for the children, knowing that at every single moment there was always someone at the hospital for Sally-Anne.

For a while she was on the maximum dose of drugs and kept sedated but every now and again doctors would shine a light into her eyes to see if they responded. They did. Sally-Anne was obviously still very much in residence. In a bizarre contradiction, Sally-Anne never looked ill throughout all these traumas, cosmetically she was still beautiful, with lovely skin and a good colour.

Seven days after Black Wednesday, when I had been told to say my last goodbye to my wife, I was at home when out of the blue came a telephone call telling me Sally-Anne wanted to see me. For the staff, to have someone nearly dying on the Wednesday then wanting to be on the phone a few days later was almost unheard of. When I arrived, she couldn't talk properly but I found some words she had written in a spidery hand like an old person's. It was unbelievable. She was desperate to have a mobile. Later I realized that when she had a phone with her, she felt safe.

Sally-Anne: I was very anxious to have a phone because I wanted to be in touch but they wouldn't let me have one in Hull. When I did get one at last, I never stopped ringing Simon.

Simon: After nearly dying on October 10th, Sally-Anne was sat out in a chair beside her bed on October 18th. The long, painful and at times tortuous journey back to health had begun. Sally-Anne despised that chair because, feeling so exhausted and battered, all she wanted was to lie still. The doctors and nurses had other ideas. Unable to speak, she wrote and wrote, though desperately slowly. There were days when she couldn't even manage that.

Having hit rock bottom, it was going to be a long climb up and she faced many setbacks. Anyone undergoing prolonged anaesthetics and traumatic brain surgery is prone to depression and on some days Sally-Anne was very low. While the rest of us had witnessed her near death and were ecstatic that she was still with us, Sally-Anne was only just waking up to what had happened. For someone who had always loved talking, it was frustrating to be able only to communicate on paper or by gestures.

The medical advice and the feeling in our own hearts was that the children shouldn't visit at this point. We thought it would be too traumatic on both sides. Once our friend Emma returned with her family to their own home, she and many other people came in to help me look after them.

By October 28th I realized Sally-Anne was improving when she gave me a right b******ing for being late but we were by no means out of the woods.

Towards the end of October a lumber puncture revealed blood still leaking from the brain and she was back into theatre again. Shortly after coming out, they whisked her in again when she failed to wake up and was found to be suffering from a clot. The bone flap in her head was on and off like a barn door in the wind but at no point did I believe I would lose her. I thought, "This is just typical of Sally-Anne. Bloody awkward!"

I wouldn't even say I was worried. She was never one to do things conventionally. She had always been disorganized, with too many things going on, always the last one to arrive anywhere and the last to leave. So I wasn't surprised at these latest developments because if anyone could be awkward, Sally-Anne could.

For about a week she was back in intensive care and on a ventilator again, sedated and out of action. Expecting to see someone with a head wrapped up like an Egyptian mummy, I was yet again surprised at the small bandage and her still pretty if rather pale face. They hadn't even had to shave off all her hair, only a little. She had no idea I was there but I sat next to her, telling her all that was going on at home with the children and the farm, that they had been going round the village on Halloween doing trick or treat.

Slowly they allowed her to come round but at the beginning of November she was in and out of theatre to drain fluid. To help her to breathe they performed a tracheotomy where a tube is inserted into the throat and until that was changed, she was unable to speak. At least she couldn't tell me off!

I spent many hours at the hospital, just sitting, waiting, drinking machine coffee out of plastic cups, walking to the stairwell where I was allowed to make calls, then sitting again, watching staff arrive for their shift and then seeing them leave to go home again. Relatives of other seriously ill patients wondered about with anxious, helpless expressions. It was good to have so many supportive people back home who were willing to listen to me and who I could talk things over with. But for all the help we received from many people, I longed to get back to our normal domestic routine. A nanny came to work for us who was marvellous and took a lot of weight off my shoulders but she was a great one for lists and strict routines and I don't do that. I was grateful but wanted my wife back again.

Charles, being the older of our two children, grew frustrated and there were some fraught scenes as I left for the hospital without taking him with me. "I want to see my Mummy! I want to come!" he'd yell, but the doctors still thought it unwise and so I did as I was told. When Charles got upset, Lucy would come out in sympathy and they'd both be screaming their heads off. Driving away from those struggling figures was heartbreaking.

One of the side effects of the aneurism was a series of strokes which affected Sally-Anne's movement and speech and no-one could tell how long term those effects would be. About the first week in November, Sally-Anne was out of intensive care and back in the high dependency ward. She was sitting up in her chair, much to my relief and to her dismay. Weak and tired, still being fed through a tube, she found even that small exercise exhausting.

Seeing my high-spirited, chatty wife slumped silently concerned me but one of the consultants had a long chat with me and he filled me with confidence. He was used to seeing people look like this at the start and knew the progress they could make. At one visit I noticed Sally-Anne had managed to remove a stray eye-lash from her eye and that tiny achievement boosted my hopes. The day came when the large pipe helping Sally-Anne to breathe was replaced by a smaller one and she could speak again. As she rasped out a few words, I felt the tears in my eyes.

A tiny valve and draining pipe was inserted into Sally-Anne's head as a permanent solution to the build up of fluid and it's still there, magnetically adjusted to slow down or speed up as needed. Towards the end of November came the welcome news that she was well enough to move back to York Hospital which perked both of us up no end and, as the stretcher was hoisted into the ambulance, she wrote a note to the crew, "Just take me home!" If only.

Sally-Anne: Before we talk about the time in York, I'll add in the bits I remember from being in Hull Hospital. I remember the sound of pouring rain, then my friend Emma standing over me, stroking my face and saying that she and her husband had moved into Ivy House Farm to look after the children. She brought her own children with her, who were great friends with Charles and Lucy. It was a very brave thing to do. Later I heard that one of the nurses had told her, "It's wrong to suggest Sally-Anne will recover because she won't" and Emma just said, "You don't know this girl, she'll pull through." Lots of other people were also helping, arriving with meals and so on, among them our friend Wendy who was a superstar.

Simon told me, "When I was driving away from the hospital, not knowing if my wife was going to make it through the night, I'd get home and find my children had been bathed and put to bed and I had someone to talk to over a glass of wine and I was very grateful." We will both be indebted to Emma and Martin for all our lives and that goes for a lot of friends and family. Coming round that

41

first time in hospital was like waking up with a thundering hangover. I felt so tired and scared and was desperate to know how the children were. I couldn't bear to have Simon out of my sight and wanted a phone with me all the time so I could always be in touch but wasn't allowed to have one for a long time.

The nurses were very kind, stroking my face. I remember very little else about my weeks in Hull but have a clear memory of waking up after an operation and seeing Simon with his head in his hands. I spoke to him and heard him say, "Sally-Anne, it hasn't gone very well. You've had a stroke." That was devastating because I didn't know how I was going to be. I thought, "Life is never going to be the same again" and I just prayed. Simon told me, "Everybody is praying for you" and that was a great comfort.

Silly things stick in my mind, like I'd not long got a new car and one of the nurses had the same one and we talked about that. I could see people sitting on my bed and hear them talking. "We've seen the children, they're ok," I heard. "You've got to get better for the children, you've got to get out of here."

So many kind people wanted to see me that Simon, on the advice of the doctors, drew up a rota of visitors, mainly family, who would make sure I was never alone. Simon and the doctors didn't want the children to see me as it would have upset them so much and it would have upset me too. It makes me cry just to think about it now.

Simon: Getting out of the specialist unit at Hull had been such a huge target that we hadn't given much thought about what the next stage would be like. It turned out to be very tough. Ward 39 at York Hospital was the acute stroke unit. Lined up in the beds or propped up in chairs were some very sad cases and we wondered what the future held for some. With the best will in the world, it was a dispiriting place for a young woman to be and Sally-Anne craved visitors to boost her flagging spirits. I drew up a rota and stuck it on our fridge at home so she wouldn't have a crowd one day and no-one the next.

It was extremely hard to leave her there but was the best thing. I never classed myself as in charge. The doctors and nurses were telling me what to do, I was just steering the ship. If they told me to turn left I turned left and just did what they said right the way through. If they said no visitors, she needed rest, that was how it had to be. If they said she could have visitors, they could come. They were the professionals and I wanted to stay focused. Hull Hospital had saved Sally-Anne from death but in York she had to learn to live again.

Chapter Six

Simon: Arriving back at York Hospital, Sally-Anne faced a long battle to regain basic skills like walking. At first she was still being fed on a drip. It was a big moment on December 6th when a nurse fed her two teaspoonsful of pureed food and half a cup of hot chocolate.

Sally-Anne: I soon got back into the swing of eating. Despite being off solids for so long, I hadn't lost weight as the drip supplied enough calories to keep things constant, which was a shame!

Simon: Charles and Lucy hadn't seen their mother since October 5th. It was now December 8th and at last I announced to them that they could see Mummy again. Sally-Anne's Auntie Joan came with me to help for it was going to be a big day for everyone. Walking into that rather oppressive atmosphere, they had eyes only for their mummy and were soon cuddling up with her on the bed.

Clever Joan had brought make-up and Lucy was soon sprucing up Sally-Anne's face. Charles was curious about everything. What were the staff doing? What was all the equipment for? Watching them, I felt a surge of relief. It was as if they had never been apart. We had both been worried about how they'd react, that they might be scared but they weren't.

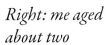

Right: me aged about two

Left: this portrait was given to the people nearest and dearest to me the Christmas after I was taken ill to remind us all of happier times and the good health I was fighting to regain

Simon and me on our wedding day

With bridesmaids Meggie (left) and Lucy

At Ivy House Farm with Charles and Lucy

Our lovely children

Left: with Charles during a visit by The Queen to Ripon in 2004. She came straight up to him and said, "Thank you for coming." He was thrilled.

Below: me with Lucy

Unable to speak, I tried to write down my thoughts in hospital

Above: with Lucy just after I had come out of hospital

Left: more of my writing from hospital, showing how vital prayer was to me

With our friend Wendy, one of those who helped us through our traumas

With our pony in 2012

At home with our two dogs Bertie and Pippa in 2012

Sally-Anne: Seeing the children for the first time after so long was both heart-warming and heart-breaking. I'd longed for them but two bundles of energy reminded me of how weak I still was. They were only six and three. We'd been worried they might be scared to see me in hospital but it was me who was scared of them.

Charles came in and said in his little voice, "Hello Mummy." He'd had a rough time and I felt I'd really let them down. One little boy had gone up to him in the playground and said, "Your Mummy's going to die." Lucy, being only three, was much less aware of the seriousness of the situation. But I didn't weep and carry on in front of them. Auntie Joan was so upbeat with them and painted Lucy's nails.

The children were fascinated by all the things around me. Lucy decided she wanted to be a nurse and wanted to help round the ward. She was a very busy girl and I started fretting about her getting lost because there wasn't much I could do about it. I got tired easily and felt so helpless and useless. After a few hours Simon told them Mummy was tired and it was time to go home. I felt awful to see their little figures disappear out of the door.

Simon: After that I took them with me most evenings and they got to know the staff, sitting at the nurses' station and asking question after question. Seeing the children reminded Sally-Anne of the person she had been, fit and energetic, and brought sharply into focus the problems she had to overcome. It didn't help that most of the others on the ward were more than twice her age but it was, from the point of view of physiotherapy and general care, the very best place for her. The consultant was Dr Elizabeth Iverson, renowned by her peers as one of best in her field, and I put all my faith in her and her team. Sally-Anne was wheeled in there in the November and walked out in the February through her own determination and everyone else helping her along.

Sally-Anne: My memory is still rather muddled after the move to the acute stroke ward in York in November. I had to learn to do things all over again – walking, talking properly, dressing, washing, making a sandwich. My occupational therapist Lois and I clicked immediately and that was a major factor in my recovery.

At first I couldn't eat and was on a drip. The first days were full of tests on my voice, my swallowing and all kinds of other things. They forced me to sit for a long time in a chair when I'd much rather have lain in bed but it was the first step in strengthening my muscles. I hated it, I felt so tired. "Is it time yet?" I'd be hollering every five minutes. I was a pain. The nurses were fantastic, patient and kind but firm about the things they knew were essential.

When Simon wasn't there, I was desperately anxious and felt lost without a phone to link me to the outside world which seemed such a remote place now but they wouldn't let me have one at that stage.

Every now and again a strange but kindly face would appear at my bedside, one of the religious people who visit hospitals offering comfort, prayers and texts to anyone wanting them. From one lovely lady I bought a wooden cross and from then on hugged it to me for comfort. Above the bed hung a washing line of photographs of the children, of me, of Simon, letters and cards. In a little black clutch bag I kept by me were some architectural drawings of Headlands, the house we wanted to build, which I'd look at and think, "I hope that happens."

Thanks to Simon's rota, which now could have a lot more names on it, I had a visitor every lunchtime and every evening until I came out. By now the prolonged stress was taking its toll on my husband. Every time he sat down at home he fell fast asleep but never missed visiting time. Christmas was speeding towards us and he had hundreds of geese to prepare for the table, spending two days up to his neck in feathers. I surprised him by remembering an order from months before about which he'd forgotten completely. It was a reassuring clue that my memory was still intact.

We had many happy memories of past Christmas Days. My favourite meal of the year is Christmas lunch with one of our own geese. Simon cooks it like nobody else and he was determined that this Christmas would be as good as it possibly could. After leaving my bedside on Christmas Eve, he stayed up for hours making preparations and didn't get to bed until after 2am. Then he was up again at 6.30am as the children attacked their stockings and because he had a goose to cook.

Christmas was brought to York District Hospital and it was brought big-style. Our wonderful friend Wendy had been out and bought the children presents, wrapped them and put them in sacks because Santa was making a special extra delivery to the hospital. It makes my cry to think about it.

At lunchtime Simon appeared in the ward carrying my best oval serving dish on which sat a goose cooked to perfection, surrounded by roast potatoes and all the trimmings. The hospital kitchen provided the vegetables and all the nurses were really excited. "We've never had goose before!" they said. We sat round the table and ate this wonderful feast.

After leaving me about 3.30pm, Simon went to his parents and then on to mine so both sets of grandparents could see the children. Afterwards he took them home and shot back to York for evening visiting. I just don't know how he did it.

Christmas was a bright spot in a gruelling time for all of us. With the help of Gareth, my physiotherapist, I had to learn to walk again. From the ward I would be wheeled in my chair into the physiotherapy room where two parallel bars stood on which I had to balance myself and try to move my reluctant feet. It was such hard work. I felt pathetic.

But I wasn't going to give up and one day, with Simon, the children and some friends there for the occasion, I walked the entire length of these bars, about three metres, and I felt euphoric, as if I'd completed a marathon. They were all clapping and cheering and Simon says I had a big grin on my face.

Washing progressed from bed baths to showers in a wheelchair and then on my feet. My co-ordination was all to pot and when they tried to teach me to blow-dry my hair, I couldn't manage it. From early on Simon had contacted a friend of mine who was a hairdresser and said, "Can you come in and sort Sally-Anne out? She looks a mess" and it boosted my self esteem to look presentable. It was a step toward the normal, the ordinary.

Clothes were just baggy tops and jogging bottoms and at first I couldn't even put those on myself. Putting on a bra was a challenge. Gradually I had to learn it all again, just as small children do, and gradually I was starting to do more and more things for myself. Mind you, I still get my knickers the wrong way round sometimes but don't we all?

Some of my memories are a bit mixed up because later I went to a rehabilitation unit, so apologies if I've got some of the events in the wrong place, but considering I nearly died, I think I'm doing pretty well. In the kitchen I had great success. Lois, the occupational therapist, would ask, "What are you going to make today?" The day I made a ham salad sandwich for Simon, standing on my own two feet, you'd think I'd cooked a gourmet meal. He was so thrilled.

I was absolutely desperate to get out and that was an incentive. Every time I saw the consultant I'd ask, "How much longer?" Simon fought tooth and nail to make sure I reached the targets which would lead to my release. Dr Iverson and her team were fantastic. The reason I am as well as I am today is because of her.

A staging post was the little flat at the end of the ward with its own bedroom and shower room where you had to prove your independence before getting parole. As I grew stronger we started going for lunch each day at The Mallards restaurant in the hospital, with me being pushed in a wheelchair. I was determined to show I could be independent because all I could focus on was getting out. I had no idea of how hard it would be when I did get out.

On New Year's Eve Simon came in to see me and said, "This is going to be our year!" Having grabbed that less than one per cent chance of surviving, we were going to make the most of it and work hard together for my recovery. It was easy to say but very hard to do for it was to be years before I was back to normal. In between lay a very rocky road and it nearly broke us up. But I suppose we had faith in each other and that kept us together. That New Year's

Eve we were united in our belief in the future, that I would recover and pick up the threads of my life and that we would build our new home together, plans for which had been interrupted by my sudden illness. Every day I would pull out the drawings of the house and say, "One day, this is going to happen." I prayed that I would be there to see it finished.

After leaving the hospital, Simon went to a party and, despite being exhausted or perhaps because of it, got absolutely blathered and finally fell into bed at 4am. Farms are no respecters of hangovers and a few hours later he paid for his excesses by having to feed the calves as the rain hammered down. Then a neighbour called for help in a difficult calving and he had to do that. It was, he told me, not a good place to be on the first day of the year.

Preparations began to be made for my release. The occupational therapist came out from the hospital to our home to see what modifications were needed if I was to cope. A bed was set up for me downstairs because the stairs were too much of a mountain for me to tackle.

The stage was set for a trial run at home but, no matter how much I longed to be there, I was scared by the challenge. It's easy to get institutionalized in a place so different from the real world. But we felt a lot of positive energy and I had made huge progress in just a few weeks. In the unit I was walking around, making lunch – just three months after being written off.

On January 29th, Simon's birthday, I was allowed home for a weekend. Exhilarated though I was to be there, having to be helped from the car into our home was a stark reminder of how changed I was. For a few minutes it was pandemonium as the children and our dogs all went mad.

I was desperate to see the place where we hoped to build our new house, though we were still battling for planning permission, and Simon drove me round the corner to the site. I sat looking across the wintery fields to the fabulous view beyond and imagined how it would feel to sit in an armchair in my new living room gazing out for miles and miles. After months cooped up indoors, I felt liberated, like an escaped prisoner. Despite the fact that this was just a short parole, that I'd have to go back in before my final release, I could now see the light at the end of the tunnel.

February 20th was my release date when I finally said goodbye to the stroke ward at York Hospital, sad to leave my trusted team of carers but anxious to escape its claustrophobic walls and some of its less happy patients. I just wanted life to be normal again.

Only a few months before, our home, Ivy House Farm, had been the focus for friends and neighbours gathering together for comfort in the belief that I was dying. Now, drawing up outside, I saw a line of red cardboard hearts strung out to welcome me back, which was our friend Emma's work. There was a little party to celebrate for which Emma and Wendy had each made a lasagne, which is my favourite, and there was a lot of jokey rivalry about whose would be the best.

It was so wonderful to see so many kind people there but I felt weak and useless and my overwhelming thought was, "How am I going to get through it all? How am I going to be now I'm back?"

That first night at home, to which I had been looking forward so much, I was shocked to find myself feeling lonely. Because I couldn't get upstairs, I slept in a bed which had been set up for me downstairs. The doctors had

51

told Simon I needed plenty of rest but also that he should not do everything for me. He was doing what he thought was best, he was still my general going into battle for me, but in my vulnerable state I felt insecure. Feelings like these gradually built up and put a tremendous strain on our marriage.

Despite these doubts, I made rapid progress at first and was soon able to tackle the stairs. The automatic armchair we'd bought to help me get up went unused because I could manage quite well on my own. But the physical challenges were one thing, the psychological barriers proved far more difficult to overcome. I was driven to school to pick up my children for the first time in many months and although I had been looking forward to it so much, it was hard, very hard. It was only when I had to face tasks I had done without thinking previously that I realized how weak I was still. I felt like an old woman surrounded by all these amazing young mums.

My mother wanted me to have a full time housekeeper and nanny but I knew I wouldn't get better by having everything done for me. Simon was keen that we should have enough help but not too much because that's what the doctors recommended. By mid February I managed to make Charles's favourite dinner, macaroni cheese, and that was a fabulous feeling to watch him eat it but it was extremely hard adjusting and I felt tense for much of the time. I believed I was useless and was even scared of the children because I worried that I couldn't look after them properly. I had never been a very patient person but was even more impatient with them now.

All kinds of dark thoughts went round my head, like, "How am I going to look after these children? If I had known what was going to happen to me, would I have had children and put them through this?" I was terrified it would have a long term effect on them.

Simon: Sally-Anne says I picked on her, that I was sometimes harsh but I was listening to the doctors and absorbing all they had to say. They told me it was vital for her to make progress early on as that would affect how much she would recover, so I did everything to encourage her in the difficult tasks they set her. If you looked at her today you wouldn't think anything was wrong with her. Only we know that Sally-Anne's health is like the blade of a knife, that it is a question now of getting that fine, sharp and shining edge to it.

Part of that was keeping at bay what I call the back-rubbing brigade, who wanted to do everything for Sally-Anne even though the doctors were encouraging her to do things for herself. When she came out of hospital she couldn't even dress herself properly. China got dropped or even thrown with a couple of choice words thrown in but I'd say, "Let's clear it up and start again." She had to keep doing it and not have things done for her all the time.

Sally-Anne: My children had been through so much that I wanted to be their mother again and was frustrated when I couldn't do it properly. I couldn't take them upstairs for a bath, make their beds or put their clothes on hangers. I was suffering from something called dyspraxia which made it feel as if I was trying to do everything while drunk. My body wouldn't move as I wanted it to and I couldn't even comprehend everything I saw. For example, I couldn't tell if the children's clothes were inside out or not, or even my own clothes, for that matter. I felt as if I had a permanent hangover.

My medical care continued with a team of experts coming to the house and us visiting the consultant in hospital when required. They kept telling me that everything I was experiencing was normal and that the more I did for myself, the better things would get but I found it so hard to accept. I convinced myself that I couldn't do things.

I kept praying and, as soon as I could, I started going to prayer groups again and that was a source of friction between Simon and me because he felt that if I had the energy for that, I could do more for myself at home. He didn't understand that being part of a prayer group was easy and being a mum wasn't because I felt I couldn't do that job properly. I felt as if someone had taken a sledgehammer to my life and smashed it to pieces. I was desperate and believed that I no longer had a job at home and was no longer needed.

I began to fall out with people who had been kind to me. I'd like to say I was very grateful but I was jealous. Before my illness I'd always had a great sense of humour, could deal it out and take it. People were used to saying outrageous things to me and hearing me laugh, as they intended. Now that I was ill, much of that robustness left me and I was sensitive to every nuance. I imagined my place had been taken at home and I felt very threatened. Had I been stronger and in a clearer state of mind I'd have put this into proportion. I was finding it hard to get back into the fold because I had been away for such a long time and still had a long way to go to recover fully. There were times when I felt no longer wanted.

I just couldn't cope when the children misbehaved, as

children often do. They were little monkeys but children are at that age. It's hard to cope with when you're a hundred per cent and I was far from that. It wasn't their fault that their Mum was a grumpy old thing. I apologize for that now. I had a friend who had cancer and who lost her battle. She was an amazing mum and used to come to see me every week in hospital. I used to think afterwards, why has she been taken and not me?

It was horrendous. I even started to think my husband didn't want me anymore. In my desperate state, I asked myself, "Why has he fought tooth and nail for me just to be like this now?" Looking back to that very dark place I can say that I really don't feel like that anymore.

Chapter Seven

After the initial euphoria of getting home, things had gone downhill badly, probably more in psychological terms than physical. I had always had a battle with my weight, my illness had done nothing to change that and I now convinced myself that Simon was getting back at me for being fat and foul in the years before. We weren't the first couple to be split asunder by prolonged stress. Where was that feeling of togetherness at New Year? I felt my life was not worth living.

Simon: There was so much positive energy about and so many people helping. Sally-Anne had been next-door to death and I wanted us to focus on the home things, not religion. I wasn't interested in the back rubbers who turned up every three weeks and offered to make tea. When I suggested Sally-Anne should make the tea instead, they looked at me as if I was a nasty person but doing these small tasks was important to her recovery. That's what the doctors were telling us and I wasn't going to argue. She needed people telling her that she could do things, not that she couldn't. She says I had unrealistic expectations of her.

Sally-Anne: At the time I wasn't thinking clearly at all. I was blind to how I was behaving but you don't tend to do things you find hard, do you? I've probably been like that all my life. After such great strides when I first arrived home, I just sat in a chair most of the time. My motivation and drive had gone and I felt I couldn't do anything.

With my recovery stalling, we went to see the neurosurgeon early in June and they decided to refer me to a specialist rehabilitation unit called Daniel Yorath House near Leeds for about six months where I would stay during the week, coming home at weekends. The work they do there is fantastic but the other patients were in a far worse state than I was, so it got me down. Simon thought I didn't need all this and the problem was that I had given up on myself. Being back among such seriously ill and injured people would be detrimental to my state of mind, he believed.

But the tide was against him and on July 22nd off I went, feeling awful about it. Simon had fought tooth and nail to get me out of hospital and I had put myself back in. All these other mums were doing a marvellous job with my family and I was just a useless piece of rubbish.

Now my week days were taken up with physiotherapy, occupational therapy and psychology. It was another institutional regime but they were very kind and made me do things, for example you had to clean your own room. All this time I was feeling desperate for my marriage to work again and I was determined not to give up. I used to walk round the gardens and pray. I had to put my trust in God because I believe He chose Simon and I to be the parents of Lucy and Charles and I didn't want my children to come from broken Britain. My faith was a huge support but it was only me that could turn things round. I used to look at my favourite photo of Simon and me with the children and think, "You selfish, horrible woman!" At home for the weekends, for all my good intentions, I still found the physical and mental demands of small children very tough. I loved them so much but felt a failure when I couldn't cope. My faith was still causing friction between me and Simon because I'd go off to church every Sunday and he saw that as time better spent with Lucy and Charles. Our disagreements weren't just about my religion for I admit I was going out socialising as well and Simon took that to mean I had no interest in the family. The truth was much more complicated. I found being a mum under my new circumstances very difficult.

At the end of my scheduled stay at Daniel Yorath House, I didn't feel any different and Simon felt there had been no improvement. People kept telling us I was loads better but they were mainly what Simon called the back rubbers and I certainly didn't feel any different.

I wasn't allowed to drive and felt I could do nothing very well at all. I still couldn't manage the co-ordination of blow-drying my hair and every single thing was a huge effort, physically and mentally, requiring a lot of concentration. It was too easy just to not bother trying.

This second homecoming was tougher than the first. When I was in the stroke unit at York, I genuinely couldn't do things. Simon and the staff were great at encouraging me to keep trying and that day I made a sandwich was a huge boost. Now it was more a psychological battle.

After I came out of Daniel Yorath in December 2008, we took a family holiday to Lapland in the hope that the magic of Santa might sprinkle something good into our troubled world. It was a disaster. Arriving at the airport in Finland, immigration officials spotted that Charles's

58

passport expired the day after and kept us waiting for ages before letting us in. Then our son went down with a terrible bug which kept him in bed and he saw precious little of Lapland. I was devastated. Lucy and I went to see Father Christmas and the reindeer and it was lovely but it would have been so much more special if it could have been the four of us. Hearing of our son's plight, Father Christmas came to the hotel room with presents and it was amazing to see Charles's face.

Back home as 2009 dawned, I began to realize what a long journey there was still ahead of me and wondered if I would ever get there, wherever there was. Before that day when I bent down to the washing machine and was struck by a devastating pain in my head, I had shedloads of confidence. Now my certainties were in shreds.

Physically, I could do most things but found everything exhausting. Because I looked alright, it was a silent illness. Expectations of me were very high but that has to be balanced against the fact that perhaps if I hadn't been prodded and pushed, I wouldn't be as well as I am now. I had always been happy in a muddle before but now couldn't function in one. Everything that required co-ordination and order was hard.

The children and I had all longed to be together again but as with all dreams like this, the reality couldn't match the expectation. I couldn't cope with any naughtiness and, being so young, Lucy and Charles began to realize this. One evening they were in the bath, not doing as they were told, and I was starting to lose my rag. Charles said, "She's going! She's going!" Then I blew my top. "She's gone!" he shouted in triumph.

I had to re-bond with them and eventually accept the

responsibility of being in sole charge of them. It was a big step forward when Simon felt confident enough to leave me alone with them, knowing I'd cope. Having coped once, I knew I could do it again. They are amazing kids and I love them very dearly but at first they took advantage of the situation. That's what children tend to do, so I'm not blaming them.

The simple skill of shopping in a supermarket had to be relearned. Wendy or other friends drove me there. Being so little, Lucy looked on the person who drove the car as the boss and that was very hurtful, though not anyone's fault. She was adapting herself to all the problems she had faced but when she wanted to hold their hand instead of mine I felt very left out. Now she holds my hand and gives me cuddles but for a while I felt as if I was a stranger to my own daughter.

Supermarkets held a special horror because I needed to know exactly what I wanted and where it was. Before, I would have flown round chucking things into the trolley. As for packing it all into bags at the end as items flew down the conveyor belt, that was beyond me. All the time I had the worry, "Is it my illness or am I just a useless person?"

It's impossible to explain to anyone who hasn't had a stroke what it felt like at times - exasperation, exhaustion and a feeling of, "I can't do this gig" were all pervading. That's when I had to sit down and really pray.

Chapter Eight

Before I go on with my story, I want to say a bit more about my faith. I have a burning ambition to abolish the stigma that surrounds it. People are scared because they've never felt it. Perhaps the reason I feel it so strongly is because of where I've been. I always knew something very nasty was going to happen to me. I had had a very nice life with no knocks at all and I think I needed a short sharp shock, being a spoilt little madam who'd always been looked after, first by my parents and then by my husband.

My faith is a huge comfort to me through all the trials of life. I don't want to force anyone to be religious, that would be impossible, but I would like them to listen with an open mind to what it has done for me. A reality exists within me of God with his son Jesus at one side and the Holy Spirit at the other and they are always there.

If you ask me what the Holy Spirit is, I have to say that I don't really know but when you connect it's like walking on air. It's a feeling which engulfs you, the difference between being able to manage and not. Faith can change your day. Suddenly it feels as if you can cope with what's being thrown at you. He always gives you the tools.

An example I can give happened not so long ago when I had to go into an unfamiliar supermarket on my own. It was late afternoon, we had eight people coming for dinner that night and not a thing was ready. I had been "God bothering", as Simon would put it, near Pickering and had to find a shop nearby, which I didn't relish. I prayed for help and went round the aisles without a hitch, returning to produce a dinner of which I was proud. I pulled it off – with help.

The power of the Holy Spirit is very strong, better than all the booze I've sunk over the years. People can't believe I hardly drink any more, just half a glass of champagne for a toast now and again. Having gone from a good-time girl to almost a teetotaller, I don't miss the alcohol at all because I'm getting a buzz from something more genuine. But I'm not trying to get everyone on the wagon, it's what works for me.

When I was in the Daniel Yorath rehabilitation unit, I had despaired of the future, not knowing how I would get back to a normal life. Walking round the garden, I told myself, "There is only one person who is the author of our journey and that's Jesus and you just have to trust that He will come through for you. Just hand yourself over to Him and have that faith." I couldn't have pulled this round without Him. Every day something good happens to me but that's partly because I appreciate small things more. Mostly we are too preoccupied to notice, worrying about what we haven't got.

While I have no doubts about God, I have huge doubts about myself. Maybe I'm just a big fraud because sometimes I blow my top and then think, "How can you scream and shout like that and call yourself a Christian? Jesus wouldn't do that." Sometimes I say things I shouldn't and afterwards think, "Your mouth is so dangerous and always has been."

Luckily for me, God loves and forgives sinners who feel sorry.

God won't barge into your life uninvited because he's not like that. He's rather understated. I feel sorry for anyone who doesn't have faith because I couldn't have got through this without it. I talk to him all the time. Sometimes I think, "I can't do this on my own" and then tell myself not to be stupid because I'm not on my own. Some people think that's ridiculous but for me it is a genuine foundation.

Going to church with the children is one of the things I love doing best. On Mother's Day I was the only one there with her children and that made me feel so sad. Little bouquets had been made by members of the congregation for children to give to their mothers but there was only me. It was a tragedy. If anybody has a problem, the church is an amazing place, both the building and the people within. After a service, I feel uplifted.

When I was at boarding school, we had to put on our Sunday suits and go off to church where I'd sit bored out of my head. If I could hide and get out of it, I would. Now I think, "What a waste! You silly girl, all those sermons you missed full of things which would have helped you!" But it was cool to be bored by God. The school, which was Methodist, had a wonderful chaplain but I would just switch off. Today I listen and learn. I hope any young person reading this will at least give it a try. It's easy to learn when you're listening.

I am a Christian because that is what I was brought up to, the same as someone else might be brought up as a Muslim, a Hindu or whatever else. I don't want to try to convert people to a different religion, it is faith that is important. You have to believe. I look at people sometimes and think,

"Faith could really help you" but I don't beat them over the head with The Bible. The only thing I can do is show what it does for me. I just know God is going to get me where I want to go.

Praying doesn't have to be down on your knees. I like to close my eyes and put my hands together but that's not always possible. I always say grace before meals, even though it embarrasses my family, because I think we should appreciate the food in front of us. People can feel disappointed if they pray for something but don't get it. God doesn't give us things willy-nilly, he does it when it's right and meant to be, so if there's no instant response to prayer that doesn't mean he's not listening.

Prayer can be very powerful. When I was in the hospital and not expected to live, Ruth texted people she knew asking them to pray for me, they in turn texted others and it spread out into a huge web of people who had never even heard of me but were praying for my recovery. That was amazing.

A book I find an inspiration and a comfort is, Daily Wisdom for Mothers: A Daily Devotional Journal by Michelle Medlock Adams, published by Barbour. Each day has a quotation from the Bible followed by her own writing about being a mum, which is unbelievably real and reflects what every mother goes through.

I feel I have a calling to help spread God's word. After all, look at what he's done for me. Some people say, "It was the surgeons!" but who was working with the surgeons? Despite being called a Bible basher and God botherer and other insults, I still feel many people want him and need only the right introduction. I take heart from the fact that a small paperback edition of the New Testament published to celebrate the Queen's Diamond Jubilee began with a very small print run but has since gone up to 600,000 copies because of demand.

For me, the one-time-ladette, faith has been a calming influence. Over dinner recently, someone asked if my faith had changed me in any way and Simon replied, "She's not as savage as she was!" I thought, no I'm not but I do have eruptions of anger and hate myself for it but they don't happen as they once used to.

A lot of people out there are interested in faith and I now have the confidence to talk about my own. I'm not embarrassed any more, feeling proud to be a Christian. If people don't want to be my friend because of it, that's their problem. If they avoid me because they think I'm some sort of nutter, I can only say, I am not a nutter, I am somebody who needs faith in her life and couldn't get through without it.

Chapter Nine

Returning to the story of my recovery, 2009 was a very tough year for Simon on the farm, juggling work and home, with the weather against him and a malevolent bull which broke three of his ribs. To cap it all, in April I had an epileptic seizure as I was walking into the house, though I had no idea what it was at the time and was terrified that I'd suffered another aneurism.

I was carrying my handbag and suddenly my fingers felt strange. The next thing I remember is waking up on the patio flagstones. I must have been thrashing about because my face was a mess. My mother was with me and drove me straight to York Hospital where I was admitted while they found out what had happened. We were relieved when scans showed no bleeding in the brain.

From early on in my illness, I had been on anti-seizure medication but at Daniel Yorath the dose had been reduced in the hope of improving my cognitive skills. Now the dose was upped again and we realized I wasn't going to be driving again for a long time, which is no joke living in the country.

In other ways, I think I got better too quickly but then I had to because I had two small children, a busy husband and we had a new house to build together. Things were still very strained between Simon and me, with lots of rows. He had had enough of my nastiness and one day stunned me by

66

saying that he wanted out. He thought I wasn't interested in family life but it wasn't that, I just couldn't cope.

Despite all these troubles, my faith was getting stronger and stronger and I was praying for the tools to be a better mum and a better wife. I believe God puts people into your life when you need them and one day after this devastating revelation, our new vicar arrived. That was a turning point for us. He walked into my kitchen, introduced himself and then got straight to the point. He said, "I hear that you guys might need a bit of help. It sounds like you've been through a very rough time." I could hardly believe this helping hand had arrived out of the blue. I told him, "We so need your help." He and his wife were better than any marriage guidance, very kind and helpful. Simon got on quite well with him and they even went out for a beer. Our divorce was on hold.

As I grew stronger, I became increasingly frustrated by my inability to drive. Instead we bought a bicycle which I had painted bright pink. It had an electric motor for the hills and for the next two years I went everywhere on that.

In one way the seizure was a big setback but in another the exercise on the bike was good for me. Maybe that was the tipping point when I gradually began to do more for myself and rediscovered some self confidence and motivation. Despite making all kinds of plans for our divorce, Simon and I didn't get round to doing anything concrete, thank goodness.

Dark thoughts still invaded my mind from time to time but now I felt I could say, "Get out, Satan! You've been running my life for too long. No more! This is not happening to me any more!" I saw these negative feelings as a malevolent invasion of my spirit and wanted to fight them. A milestone was passed the day I cycled with Charles and Lucy to church. We arrived early and the warden asked them if they'd like to ring the bell and put up the hymn numbers. These were small, ordinary things but it was an ordinary that I had feared might never happen again. Tears ran down my face because I couldn't believe I was sitting in church with my children either side of me.

Over the next two years both my physical and my mental strength returned but very slowly and there were lots of ups and downs. Some things have blurred and I'm not sure exactly when each of the events I am describing occurred. Looking back, I can see that it was only in the summer of 2012 that I woke up to the fact that I was, for want of a more appropriate word, better.

During my long period of recovery, we made some changes to our lives to take out some of the stresses and strains. One huge decision was to move the children from Cundall Manor to a village school much nearer because the pick-ups by car were becoming increasingly complicated as they finished at different times. Each morning Lucy and Charles were being driven through Flawith where most of the local children were queuing for the school bus and we thought, "What are we doing?"

Unable to drive myself, this inability to do the basic Mum chore of the school run was adding to my feelings of insecurity and exclusion. After their move, I could get Charles and Lucy ready in the morning myself, then walk them to the bus stop and meet them at the end of the school day. Luckily they settled in quickly and I also made new friends at the bus stop.

I hated having to rely on lifts to go anywhere myself. It was awful, I felt a burden on everybody until one day

I thought, "Why don't I just get on the bus?" Lucy and I walked to Alne Cross, boarded the service to York and by the end of the ride we knew all the passengers on that bus, because that's the sort of person I am, I talk to everyone. Lucy thought I was bonkers but forgave me when we treated ourselves to lunch in Bettys. A street performer who paints himself purple and does bike stunts captivated us for a while and afterwards he told us his own story – he was an interesting character – and I told him all about me. He said, as so many others have, "You must write a book!" It's taken me a while to get round to it.

Being in the crowded city was a tonic and released all the natural chatter inside me. I talked to the people in the queue at Bettys and the guy playing piano and Lucy said, "Mummy, do you talk to everyone?" All too soon our outing came to an end and Simon picked us up and brought us home. That was a good day for I knew I could get on the bus on my own with my child and go into York just like other mums.

Another milestone was cooking Sunday lunch for friends, roast beef with all the trimmings, which is a challenge for anyone's planning and co-ordination, but I just had to get it right and I did, with Simon's help. It was a personal triumph and made me feel really good. I thought, "I've cracked it, I can do Sunday lunch again."

Exercise has been crucial to my recovery. One of the mums I'd got to know when I took the children to the bus stop in the mornings gave me a book about running and I decided I would try it. If what I was reading was true, the weight would melt off me. I had never run before but I bought myself some trainers and just did it.

With the help of a running watch I began by running

for a minute, walking for a minute and so on, at first just up and down the yard at Ivy House Farm. When I felt ready to go further, I waited until it was almost dark before setting out so no-one would see me. At my heaviest, I had been over 19 stone and even though I had by that time dropped down to about 16 stone, I still didn't want people to see me jogging along. I managed half a mile that first evening and felt very proud.

Before I was ill, Simon never once commented on my size, even when I got really big. Afterwards, that changed. At first I took this very hard, as a sign that he didn't want me, but now see that he was concerned I should eat healthily because he wanted me to be well. As I was running I thought, "This will do it! This will mend things!" As I pounded the fields I thought, "If I can bring myself back from the brink of death, I can mend my marriage."

It was a long time before I really took life back into my own hands again. At the Daniel Yorath rehabilitation centre I had been advised not to swim because of the epilepsy. Understandably, most professionals were unwilling to commit themselves when I asked anything like, Can I run? Can I swim? There was a certain amount of buck passing. In the end I had to make my own decisions and took the plunge, literally. Getting into a swimming pool again was liberating and left me feeling glowing.

I got used to having the occasional seizure, though luckily one never happened in the water, and came to recognize the characteristic feeling in my hands which was the warning sign. Now I wasn't frightened of them and knew what was happening. Five minutes later I'd be fine. I haven't had one since April 2010.

For a while the running bug took hold of me and in 2011

I took part in a 10 kilometre run, which was exhilarating. Then I let things slide a bit, which is easily done with running because each run you miss makes the next one harder.

Another milestone was passed in September 2011 when I got my driving licence back. The post plopped on to the doormat and there was an envelope marked DVLA. I tore it open and saw my photo on the licence and felt elated. For someone who had always adored cars and resented being dependent on others, it was a great day. After a couple of refresher lessons the instructor said, "You're a better driver than most other people on the road."

The first drive on my own was terrifying, I was a nervous wreck but soon got used to it again. That evening I took the children out to one of their favourite places. As we drove along, Charles said in a little voice, "Mummy, I feel like I want to cry" and I thought, "How terrible this has been for them, to have a mother who was virtually housebound."

Filling up with fuel for the first time in so long was humiliating when the man in the kiosk had to announce over the tannoy what I had to do. They'd put new buttons on the pumps to select pay at pump or pay at kiosk and that tripped me up completely. I've since learned that other people have wondered why their pump wasn't working, having failed to spot the new buttons, but I was attributing every problem to my illness and felt useless. I couldn't even fill my car up.

By this time Simon and I had decided we wanted to stay together, though we were still rowing. Meanwhile, our farming business was continuing to grow and we were now keeping geese, beef cattle and a few rare breed pigs. After a long and stressful battle for planning permission, work had begun on our new home in March 2011 on the land we owned nearby and the following January we sold Ivy House Farm and moved into a mobile home next to the site.

My faith grows stronger every day though it can still be a source of friction between me and Simon. Having the joint project of the house helped to bring us together and he has worked so hard to get it finished. I'm busy choosing the kitchen, lighting, bedroom fittings, paint, curtains and the hundreds of other things a new house needs. I see it as a fresh start for us all.

As in all building projects, it has taken longer and cost more than we thought. A fortune disappeared on legal fees getting permission in the first place. Not long after I came out of intensive care Simon told me that we had been accused by those opposing our plans of trying to build a manor house. I didn't want to live in a manor! It's a traditionally designed family home.

Being a fresh site, we had to install water, electricity, phone lines and an access road. Sometimes we wished we'd never started but had dug ourselves in so deep that there was only one way out and that was to keep digging.

As we walked out of the door of Ivy House Farm for the last time, Simon said, "We've had some very happy times here and some very sad ones. We've brought two children home here and we've nearly got divorced here." I'm so glad he said it because it was all true. I love him so much.

Epilogue

If you saw me today, you would have no idea of what I've been through. I look and am fit and healthy. If I get to know you well, I might let you feel the bump on my head where the "door" was, if you really wanted to. At the time of writing this book, it is five years since I was struck down by that first blinding headache while loading the washing machine.

Only in the summer of 2012 could I confidently say I was back to normal. I can multi-task and I can plan. Reading about dyslexia has also widened my understanding of it, making me realize how it has caused extra complications in my recovery. It can affect your personal organization and the ability to put things in order. Anyone who knows me will say I have lived in chaos virtually all my life and perhaps the dyslexia contributed to that. Simon says it's laziness but I don't think I am a lazy person.

Before I just muddled through but today I can't function without a system and am a bit worried about moving into our new house. Everything is going to have to have its place. I call myself the Mended Mess because I am getting better physically and feel stronger spiritually but I can't let down my guard for a moment. Life is now all about sticking to routines and systems.

One of the reasons for writing this book was to give inspiration to people who, like me, have spent a lifetime fighting the flab. My weight and I are old enemies but now at last I think I am winning and well on the way to my target. Exercise is a crucial element and I swim as often as I can. Being in the water fills me with an enormous feeling of freedom and I try to do 50 lengths each time, which is half a mile in that pool. I want people to feel inspired that if I can lose weight after all I've been through, they can too. I'm bound to say as well that, for me, having faith in God helps as I never feel alone in this battle.

I do my own thing on the diet front as I no longer feel the need to go to a slimming club. I have been to them all and know what I need to do – be sensible. I have regular check-ups with the doctor and the nurse at our GP practice. The nurse is a real tonic and is a believer, like me. As she says, God has done his bit, now I have got to do mine. At my heaviest I was 19st 10lb. I am now 14st 8lb and my goal before Christmas is 12st 7lb. I would love to get down to 10st one day.

In the past I always had au pairs to help but today I can manage without, though Simon does a huge amount looking after the children and the home. I couldn't manage without him or the local family whose daughters have provided a wonderful babysitting service over many years.

I have come a long way on my journey back to good health but my recovery is still continuing. It's a question of fine tuning. My co-ordination is still being sharpened. There remain milestones to be passed. The other day I washed my children's duvets and put them back on myself for the first time since I was ill. For me it was a triumph of co-ordination. I haven't tried to tackle our king-sized one yet. As our new house is being built, we are living in a mobile home through one of the wettest summers on record, surrounded by mud, which has not been easy. Being in such cramped conditions gave rise to another milestone - taking my make-up off in the dark before going to bed. I don't like turning on the bathroom light late at night to do my cleansing in case I wake the children but for a long time I just couldn't manage that simple task. Then the other evening, after memorizing where all the bottles were on the shelf, I did it.

Some things I just can't do as well as I once did, which is frustrating. Wrapping presents used to be an artistic joy for me, now I get the paper the wrong way round and can't do bows. Making things fit in envelopes is another difficulty. Going away on holiday is a challenge because I need to transfer my system from here to there and it's hard work, almost easier to stay at home. I still find technology mind-boggling and can't face doing anything on the computer but Simon thinks that's my laziness, so perhaps I should take a class.

I wouldn't have got through this without the support of Simon and my faith in Jesus. I would also like to say that my parents are the best pair of genes I've got because they're not quitters and that was another thing that helped me to survive. We don't give up and if I did for a while, I got up and got going again. I also have a team I call my angels who are people always there ready to help when needed.

Despite being so much better, my days are punctuated by a regular cocktail of drugs to keep me shipshape and the little pump in my head is still there doing its stuff. Regular check-ups and MRI scans dot my calendar.

What happened to me came out of the blue. Now, with so many scans of my brain, I know that there is a second weakness in one of my veins. Anyone can have these time bombs ticking away and go through life never knowing and without suffering the slightest problem. The doctors tell me that if my personal time bomb was going to explode, it would have done so by now but it is a salutary reminder to me to try not to waste any of the days left to me.

And what about Simon and me? We're still together and still rowing but I hope I now appreciate what a great husband he is. He used to love me unconditionally but I don't think he does anymore. Maybe that's a healthier kind of relationship but I do miss the feeling of being adored.

It's strange to say but I believe this aneurism saved my marriage. Before I was ill, I was a spoilt little cow who didn't know what a good marriage she had. If Simon hadn't pulled me up short by saying we had no future and making me appreciate what an amazing man I'd got, I would never have realized what I stood to lose. I now know that I have a need and that I am needed.

A friend asked me if my book was going to be a horror or self help! I laughed and said, "Maybe a bit of both." The best self help book available is The Bible. It's all in there so, please, if you are in a bad place and need some help, don't dismiss the power of prayer or The Church. My community have been amazing, not to mention the wonderful doctors, nurses, occupational therapists, friends and family – my angels! You know who you are. I am so very, very grateful. God bless you all. I would love to name you all individually but there isn't enough room and I would hate to miss someone out and offend them.

I really must make something of myself. I am now singing with The Yorkshire Decibelles Choir and we are available to sing at events (decibelles@sladden.com).

I am very aware that there could be someone who reads this book who has lost a loved one through an aneurism and I feel very guilty that I have lived while others have not. I am not suggesting that the reason I survived is because I am a Christian. God didn't have a job for me there, he has a job for me here. This is why I have written the book and shared our story. If in any way this book can help just one person, it has been worth it.

Every night and morning I pray that I will be the best mum and wife I can be. I am trying to create a new normal. What matters most is that I'm now back to being the Mum I wanted to be and I hope the children have forgiven me for the way I was.

Some people say I am amazing for surviving against such horrific odds but I'm not amazing. I had an awful lot of help. It's particularly hard for Simon to hear people tell me I'm amazing for having survived when he knows how much he and others were part of that miracle.

The other day I was sitting in the waiting area of Hull Hospital for a check-up and one of the neurosurgeons walked past. He recognized Simon straightaway, then did a double-take on seeing me. "Sally-Anne?" he asked in astonishment.

"Yes, I am," I replied.

Then he took me aback by asking, "Are you a full shilling?"

And, quick as a flash, I replied, "Well, I wasn't one before!"

Then came that word again, "Gosh, you're amazing!" he said. Even if not a full shilling, I hope that I am a better person than I was before. I want to make something of my life now because I have been given a second chance. It has been a rough and rocky road but with the power of prayer, you can do anything.

The Power of Prayer

Here are some verses from the Bible that help me daily.

I can do everything through him who gives me strength.

Philippians 4:13

For I know the plans I have for you, declares The Lord, plans to prosper you and not to harm you, plans to give you hope and a future.

Jeremiah 29.11

Do not let any unwholesome talk come out of your mouths, only what is helpful for building others up.

Ephesians 4:29

Love bears all things.

Corinthians 13:7

Therefore do not worry about tomorrow for tomorrow will worry about itself

Matthew 6:34

Dear children do not let anyone lead you astray.

John 3:7

Jesus answered, I am the way and the truth and the life.

John 14:6

My guilt has overwhelmed me like a burden too heavy to bear.

Psalm 38:4

Where there is no vision, the people perish.

Proverbs 29:18

Teach me to do your will for you are my God.

Psalm 143.10

God is fair and just, he corrects the misdirected and sends them in the right direction.

Psalm 25:8

And here are a few of my own prayers.

Dear Heavenly Father, help me to never lose my vision or my drive. I want to move forward with you. Amen.

Heavenly Father, please help me not to be afraid of disciplining my children. Amen.

Dear Lord, please reawaken the dream on the inside of me, the one that you placed there. Amen.